A Note F

MW00627100

I, Yoshi, along with Maste
Delicious Taste of Japan" and developed Yoshi's special sauces so that
Americans can get Japanese taste in each and every meal. You can
experience Japanese flavor any time with anything, even with leftovers such
as meat, ham, shrimp or vegetables by using Yoshi's special sauces! These
recipes are just the beginning. My easy everyday recipes and your
imagination makes any taste possible. Please try to be creative
and enjoy the delightful combinations of oriental and western
dishes that I have provided for you.

Yoshi Shioda lives in Charlotte, NC with his wife. They own the restaurant
"Tokyo" that provides authentic Japanese foods to people in
North and South Carolina.

Yoshi Shioda with Chef Fumio Ina of Restaurant Tokyo

2

Enoki Mushroom Salad

Ingredients:

2	Red Radish
1/2	teaspoon Salt
1	pack Enoki Mushrooms
4	leaves Green Leaf Lettuce
	Yoshi's Teriyaki Dressing

① Cut stems off of red radishes and slice very thin. Place radish slices in cold water for 5 minutes. Drain in a colander. (See picture ❶)

② Heat salted water until boiling. Cook enoki mushrooms for 10 seconds and drain. Place in ice water until mushrooms are chilled. (See picture ❷)

③ Drain and cut stems off enoki mushrooms. (See pictures ❸ and ❹)

④ Arrange radish and enoki mushrooms on plate. Season with Yoshi's Teriyaki Dressing to taste.

Makes 2 servings.

Note: Hot mustard goes well with Yoshi's Teriyaki Dressing.

Enoki Mushroom Salad

Cabbage Salad

Ingredients:

Cabbage
Green Leaf Lettuce
Broccoli
Tomatoes
Cucumbers
Yoshi's Teriyaki Dressing

① Cut cabbage into 4 wedges. Core each.
(See picture ❶)

② Cut each wedge into thin slices for a delightful crispy and sweet cabbage taste. (See picture ❷) Place cabbage into cold water for 5 to 10 minutes. Drain in a colander.

③ Place vegetables on plate - green leaf lettuce first, then cabbage, broccoli, tomatoes and cucumbers. Pour Yoshi's Teriyaki Dressing over them.

Makes 2 servings.

Origami (The Ancient Japanese Art of Paper Folding)
The Pigeon

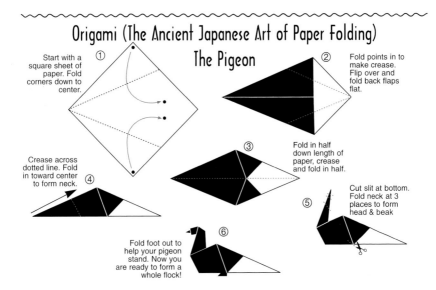

① Start with a square sheet of paper. Fold corners down to center.

② Fold points in to make crease. Flip over and fold back flaps flat.

③ Fold in half down length of paper, crease and fold in half.

④ Crease across dotted line. Fold in toward center to form neck.

⑤ Cut slit at bottom. Fold neck at 3 places to form head & beak

⑥ Fold foot out to help your pigeon stand. Now you are ready to form a whole flock!

Cabbage Salad

Mixed Vegetable Salad

Ingredients:

2   Asparagus

2   Leaves Red Lettuce

1/2 teaspoon Salt

3   Cauliflower (bite size)

2   Cherry Tomatoes

3   tablespoons Yoshi's Teriyaki Dressing

① Peel asparagus tips. If too hard, remove. (picture ❶)

② Heat salted water until boiling; add asparagus. Cook 10 seconds and drain. Place in water until cold. Halve asparagus. (picture ❷)

③ Cut lettuce and arrange vegetables on plate. Pour Yoshi's Teriyaki Dressing over them.

Makes 1 serving.

Note: This dish makes a great light meal.

Mixed Vegetable Salad

Ginger Salad

Ingredients:

            Lettuce
            Cucumbers
            Tomatoes
            Broccoli
            Celery
            Yoshi's Ginger Dressing

①   Cut lettuce and vegetables into bite size pieces and place in bowl. Top with Yoshi's Ginger Dressing.

Makes 1 serving.

Note: This dressing goes with any type of salad you wish.

Origami (The Ancient Japanese Art of Paper Folding)
The Beetle

① Start with a square sheet of paper. Fold one corner down to another. Then fold two corners down to form square.

② Fold flaps up along dotted lines.

③ Fold only ONE layer up along dotted line.

④ Fold bottom flap along dotted line to make layered folds.

⑤ Fold two sides under and two top points fold into the wings.

⑥ And now you can start a band!

Ginger Salad

Bean Sprout Salad

Ingredients:

1/2	teaspoons Salt
1/4	cup Bean Sprouts
2	leaves Green Leaf Lettuce
1	leaf Red Leaf Radicchio
2	Cherry Tomatoes
	Hot Mustard or Horseradish
	Yoshi's Teriyaki Dressing

① Heat salted water until boiling; add bean sprouts. Cook 10 seconds and drain. (See picture ❶)

② Place in cold water until chilled and drain. (See picture ❷)

③ Place vegetables on plate. Pour Yoshi's Teriyaki Dressing over them.

Makes 1 serving.

Note: Dressing also goes well with hot mustard or horseradish.

Origami (The Ancient Japanese Art of Paper Folding)
The Tiger Moth

① Fold square sheet of paper in half, corner to corner.

② Fold up only one flap to expose bottom sheet. Crease bottom sheet as shown.

Fold up bottom sheet as shown. Crease the three areas shown by the dotted lines. Fold the two sides together, then fold each wing up.

③

④ Flip over. One Tiger Moth, ready for flight!

Bean Sprout Salad

Avocado Shrimp Boat Salad

Ingredients:

1   Avocado

6   boiled Shrimp

Yoshi's Ginger Dressing

① Halve avocado and scoop out seed. Remove rest of inside with teaspoon and cut to preferred size.
(See pictures ❶,❷ and ❸)

② Halve peeled boiled shrimp (See picture ❹)

③ Mix avocado, shrimp and Yoshi's Ginger Dressing.
Fill avocado skin with shrimp mixtures. (See pictures ❺ and ❻)

Makes 2 servings.

Origami (The Ancient Japanese Art of Paper Folding)
The Butterfly

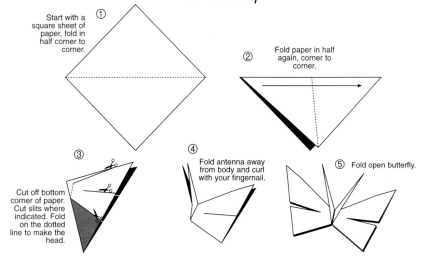

① Start with a square sheet of paper, fold in half corner to corner.

② Fold paper in half again, corner to corner.

③ Cut off bottom corner of paper. Cut slits where indicated. Fold on the dotted line to make the head.

④ Fold antenna away from body and curl with your fingernail.

⑤ Fold open butterfly.

Avocado Shrimp Boat Salad

Avocado and Ham Salad

Ingredients:

1	Avocado
1	Slice of Ham (1/2-inch thick)
	Yoshi's Ginger Dressing

① Halve avocado and scoop out seed. Skin avocado and slice thin. (See picture ❶)

② Place sliced avocado on plate. Dice ham.

③ Place diced ham in center of avocado. Season to taste with Yoshi's Ginger Dressing.

Makes 2 servings.

Origami (The Ancient Japanese Art of Paper Folding)
The Caterpillar

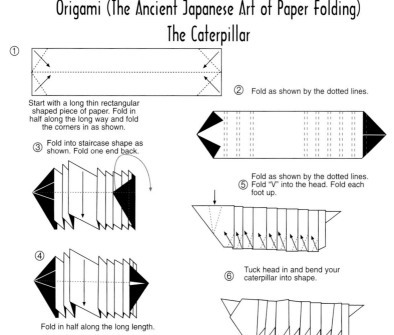

① Start with a long thin rectangular shaped piece of paper. Fold in half along the long way and fold the corners in as shown.

② Fold as shown by the dotted lines.

③ Fold into staircase shape as shown. Fold one end back.

④ Fold in half along the long length.

⑤ Fold as shown by the dotted lines. Fold "V" into the head. Fold each foot up.

⑥ Tuck head in and bend your caterpillar into shape.

Avocado and Ham Salad

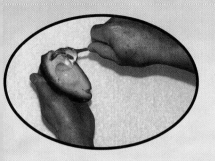

Seafood Salad

Ingredients:

2	leaves Red Leaf Lettuce
1	Snow Crab Leg
3	Shrimp
3	Scallops
3	slices Cucumber
3	Tomatoes (sliced)
4	Broccoli (sliced)

Yoshi's Teriyaki Dressing

Mustard or Horseradish

① Cut red leaf lettuce in preferred size. Place on plate.

② Boil crab leg for 20 seconds and drain. Do not dispose of hot water. Pull meat out of shell.

③ Boil shrimp with same hot water. Skin shrimp.

④ Boil scallops for 30 seconds in a separate pot. Slice in preferred size.

⑤ Place vegetables, crab meat, shrimp and scallops on plate. Pour Yoshi's Teriyaki Dressing over it. Add mustard or horseradish if you like.

Makes 1 serving.

Romaine Lettuce Salad

Ingredients:

Romaine Lettuce
Broccoli
Tomatoes
Cucumbers
Yoshi's Teriyaki Dressing

① Cut Romaine lettuce in large pieces. Cut broccoli, tomatoes and cucumbers in bite size pieces (See picture ❶).

② Place vegetables on plate. Pour Yoshi's Teriyaki Dressing over vegetables.

Makes 1 serving.

Note: You may substitute Red leaf or Green leaf lettuce.

Origami (The Ancient Japanese Art of Paper Folding)
The Swallow

①

Start with a square sheet of paper and cut it in half diagonally.

②

Fold the triangle in half corner to corner. Crease along dotted lines & fold inward to make neck and head

③

Cut off grey area and cut slit where shown. Fold wing over.

④

Slit tail and fold on dotted lines.

⑤

Fold tail and wings and the swallow is ready.

Bean Sprouts Sandwich

Ingredients:

1	cup Bean Sprouts
1	tablespoon Oil
4	tablespoons Yoshi's Teriyaki Sauce
1	teaspoon Cornstarch
2	Hot Dog Buns

① Heat frying pan. Sauté bean sprouts in oil for 1 minutes. (See picture ❶)

② Add Yoshi's Teriyaki Sauce. (See picture ❷)

③ Mix cornstarch with 2 tablespoons water. Take 1/3 starch mixture and add to bean sprouts.

④ Place bean sprouts on buns and serve.

Makes 2 servings.

Holidays & Festivals...

Setsubun (February 3 or 4): the day before the beginning of Spring by the Lunisolar calendar. On the evening of this day, people open the doors to their house and drive the bad luck out by throwing handfuls of dry soy beans and shouting "Oni wa soto, Fuku wa uchi!"("Bad luck out! Good luck in!").

Bean Sprouts Sandwich

Teriyaki Steak Sandwich

Ingredients:

3   slices Beef (thin sliced)

1   Sub Bun

    Teriyaki Dipping Sauce (see recipe below)

    Lettuce

    Tomato

    Onion

① Cook sliced beef as you like; bake, grill or fry. (See picture ❶)
② Dip meat into sauce. (See picture ❷)
③ Arrange everything on bun and serve.

Makes 1 serving.

Teriyaki Dipping Sauce

1   cup Yoshi's Teriyaki Sauce

3   tablespoons Sugar

6   tablespoons Soy Sauce

1   teaspoon Cornstarch

Place Yoshi's Teriyaki Sauce, sugar and soy sauce in pan.
Bring to a boil. Mix 2 tablespoons water with 1 teaspoon corn starch.
Mix starch mixture with sauce. (See picture ❸)

Makes 15 - 20 servings.

Teriyaki Steak Sandwich

Teriyaki Hamburger

Ingredients:

1   Hamburger Patty
1   Hamburger Bun
    Teriyaki Dipping Sauce (see Teriyaki Steak Sandwich)
    Lettuce
    Tomato
    Onion

① Cook hamburger as you like; grill or fry. (See picture ❶)

② Dip meat into sauce. (See picture ❷)

③ Arrange everything on bun.

Makes 1 serving.

Holidays & Festivals...

Tanabata (July 7): The Star Festival, is a combination of Chinese traditional holiday with beliefs peculiar to Japan. This festival celebrates the meeting, just once a year, of two star crossed lovers, Kengyu (the star Altair, the cowherd) and Orihime (the star Vega, a weaving girl), who are separated by the Milky Way (Amanogawa) on the other days of the year. Pieces of bamboo are set up in the garden and decorated with colored strips of paper, on which poems associated with the legend are written.

Teriyaki Hamburger

Stir Fry Teriyaki Green Bean Sandwich

Ingredients:

Hot Dog Buns or Sub Buns

Tomato

Cucumber

Lettuce

Onion

Stir Fry Teriyaki Green Beans

① In picture, the sandwich is made with hot dog buns.

② Cut bun and place vegetables inside. Add stir fry green beans (see recipe on page 46).

Origami (The Ancient Japanese Art of Paper Folding)
The Giraffe

① Start with a square sheet of paper fold along the dotted lines.

② Fold paper corner to corner as shown.

③ Crease two lines.

④ Fold creases in to form neck.

⑤ Cut areas indicated and fold head and nose.

⑥ Your giraffe is now ready!

Stir Fry Teriyaki Green Bean Sandwich

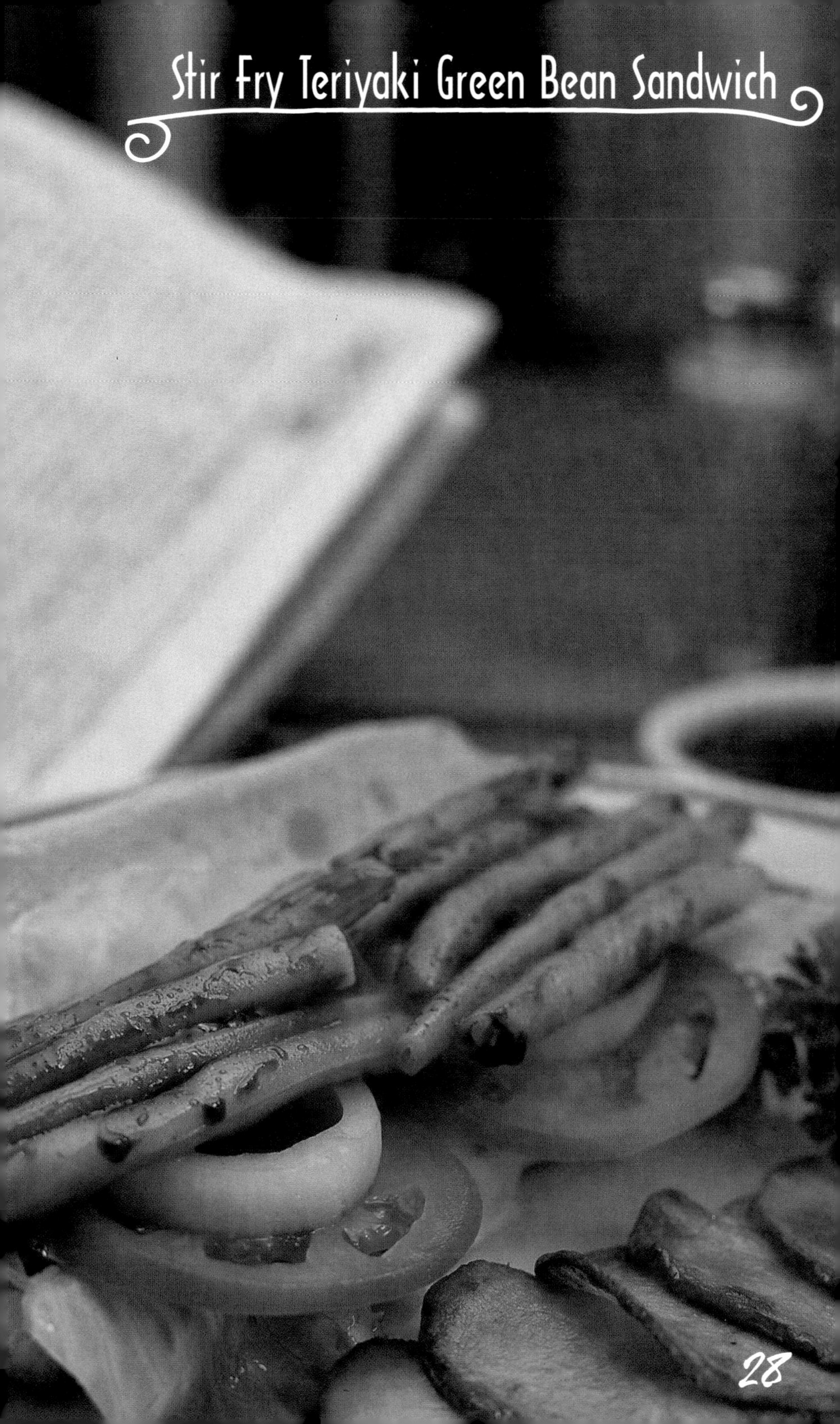

Beef & Broccoli

Ingredients:

7/8	cups Broccoli
1/2	cup Beef
8	tablespoons Yoshi's Teriyaki Sauce
1	teaspoon Cornstarch
3	tablespoons Oil

Yoshi recommends that you cook this meal one plate at a time to preserve flavor.

① Cut broccoli and beef into preferred sizes. (See picture ❶)

② Place beef in a bowl. Add Yoshi's Teriyaki Sauce (2 tablespoons). Marinate for a while. (See picture ❷)

③ Sprinkle 1 teaspoon cornstarch over beef. (See picture ❸) This will make your beef much more tender.

④ Sauté broccoli with oil (1$^{1/2}$ tablespoons) for 30-40 seconds. (See picture ❹)

⑤ Sauté beef with oil (1$^{1/2}$ tablespoons) for 20-30 seconds. (See picture ❺)

⑥ Add broccoli and 6 tablespoons Yoshi's Teriyaki Sauce. (See picture ❻) Cook for 20 seconds. Arrange on a plate.

Makes 1 serving.

Note: This dish can be made without step ② and ③, if you prefer.

Holidays & Festivals...

Tsukimi (nights when the moon is full on August 15 & September 13 of the lunar calendar): the days for "moon gazing". Decorations of Japanese pampas grass are used, and a moon-offerings of sake and Tsukimi dango (a kind of rice cake) are made as people enjoy the autumn evening and gaze at the moon.

Beef & Broccoli

Chicken and Mixed Vegetables

Ingredients:

1/2	cup Broccoli
1/2	cup Zucchini Squash
1/2	cup Onion
1/2	cup Chicken
3	tablespoons Oil
6	tablespoons Yoshi's Teriyaki Sauce
1	teaspoon Cornstarch

Yoshi recommends that you cook this meal one plate at a time to preserve flavor.

① Cut vegetables and chicken into preferred size. (See picture ❶)

② Preheat frying-pan. Sauté vegetables with oil (1¹ᐟ² tablespoons) and set aside. (See picture ❷)

③ Preheat frying-pan. Cook chicken with oil (1¹ᐟ² tablespoons) until done. (See picture ❸) Add vegetables and Yoshi's Teriyaki Sauce. Cook for 20 seconds. (See picture ❹)

④ Mix 1 teaspoon cornstarch with 2 tablespoons of water. Add 1/2 starch mixture to vegetable mixture. (See picture ❺)

⑤ Place on plate and serve.

Makes 1 serving.

Note:

Also delicious with pork, ham, or sausage.

Holidays & Festivals...

Schichi-go-san (November 15): the seven-five-three festival is when parents with boys of five, girls of seven and either boys or girls of three years old dress their children in brightly colored clothes and take them to shrines to be thankful for their children's health. These three numbers were chosen because odd numbers are considered lucky in Japan.

Fried Rice

Ingredients:

2	Scallions
2	Beef Franks
1	Egg
2	tablespoons Oil
1$^{1/2}$	cups Steamed Rice
1	teaspoon Butter
	Salt
	Pepper
2	tablespoons Yoshi's Teriyaki Sauce

① Cut scallion into small pieces. (See picture ❶) Halve beef franks. (See picture ❷) Cut into small pieces.

② Beat Egg. Cook scrambled egg with 1/2 tablespoons of oil. (See picture ❸)

③ Heat pan. Cook beef franks with 1/2 tablespoon oil for 1 minute. (See picture ❹)

④ Mix beef franks, 1 tablespoon oil, steamed rice, egg, salt, pepper, and 1 teaspoon butter.

⑤ Scoop a hole in middle. Pour Yoshi's Teriyaki Sauce in center. This will enhance the flavor of Yoshi's sauce. (See picture ❺)

⑥ Add scallions; do not over cook. (See picture ❻). Place on plate and serve.

Makes 1 serving.

Note: Also delicious with Pork, ham, or sausage.

Fried Rice

Linguine Ala Yoshi

Ingredients:

1/2	Green Bell Pepper
1/2	Red Bell Pepper
1/2	cup Onion
4	Basil leaves
10	Shrimp
2	Bamboo sticks
1	cup Linguine (or 8 ozs.)
	Salt
	Pepper
2	tablespoons Olive Oil
2	teaspoons Butter
6	tablespoons Yoshi's Ginger Dressing

① Slice green pepper, red pepper, onion and 2 basil leaves into thin strips. (See picture ❶)

② De-vein shrimp; use the tip of a knife to lift out the black vein. (See picture ❷) Thread shrimp.

③ Place 5 shrimp on each bamboo stick. This is to prevent shrimp from curling and to enhance presentation.

④ Cook linguine as directed. Drain in a colander.

⑤ Place linguine, salt and pepper in a bowl. Add olive oil. (See picture ❸) Mix them well.

⑥ Sauté onion, green and red pepper with black pepper, salt and butter. (See picture ❹)

⑦ Mix 5 and 6. Add Yoshi's Ginger Dressing and 2 basil leafs. Place mixture on plate. (See picture ❺)

⑧ Pan-fry threaded shrimp with butter. (See picture ❻)

⑨ Place cooked shrimp on top of linguine mixture. Decorate with basil leaf per plate.

Makes 2 servings.

Linguine Ala Yoshi

Marinated Mix-Oven Pot Roast

Ingredients:

1¼ cup Chicken, Beef or Pork (approx. 10 ozs.)

1 large Potato

1/4 Eggplant

1 large Onion

1 green Bell Pepper

1/2 clove Garlic

1 cup Yoshi's Teriyaki Sauce

Preheat oven to 350 degrees.

① Cut meat in large bite size pieces. (See Picture ❶)

② Skin eggplant and cut vegetables as shown. (See Picture ❷)

③ Skin garlic.

④ Boil potato for 9 minutes and drain - don't over cook. (See Picture ❸)

⑤ Mix all with Yoshi's Teriyaki Sauce. Place mixture into casserole dish (7"x7"). Marinate for 2-3 minutes. (See Picture ❹)

⑥ Bake uncovered 40 to 60 minutes until brown. Poke with bamboo stick to see if it's done.

Makes 2 servings.

Holidays & Festivals...

Obon (around mid-August): the Festival of Souls. In this festival a variety of foods are offered to the spirits of ancestors, and their rest is prayed for. People who have moved to the cities to work will return to their hometown during this festival. Most businesses close for this holiday. In towns and villages across the country people in *yukata* (light cotton *kimono*) gather for outdoor dances known as *bon-odori*. For many Japanese, summer isn't summer without a *bon-odori*.

Marinated Mix-Oven Pot Roast

Roast Beef

Ingredients:

2 1/2 lbs. Beef Roast

1/2 cup Yoshi's Teriyaki Sauce

2-4 leaves Nappa Cabbage

1   large Freezer Bag

     Hot Mustard or Horseradish

① Poke holes in beef. (See Picture ❶)

② Place beef and Yoshi's Teriyaki Sauce in freezer bag. Refrigerate for 12 to 24 hours. (See Picture ❷)

③ Place beef on top of nappa cabbage in ovenware. (See Picture ❸) Excess fat will be absorbed by the cabbage and helps to prevent it from burning.

④ Heat oven to 370 degrees. Bake for 90 minutes.

⑤ After 40 to 70 minutes, poke with bamboo stick to see if it's done. Place stick on the outside of your lower lip; if stick is cold, beef is rare. If stick is warm, beef is medium or medium rare. Take meat out when it has reached your desired doneness. (See Picture ❹)

⑥ If you like more teriyaki taste, add more Yoshi's Teriyaki Sauce mixed with cornstarch over beef and cook 400 degrees for 3 minutes before done. Cut beef to desired size. (See Picture ❺) Serve with hot mustard or horseradish.

Makes 3-4 servings.

Roast Beef

Shrimp and Mixed Vegetables

Ingredients:

1/2 cup Broccoli

1/2 cup Zucchini Squash

1/2 cup Onion

1/2 cup Shrimp

3 tablespoons Oil

6 tablespoons Yoshi's Teriyaki Sauce

1 teaspoon Cornstarch

① Cut vegetables in preferred size. De-vein shrimp; use tip of a knife to lift out the black vein. (See picture ❶)

② Preheat frying-pan. Sauté vegetables with oil (1 1/2 tablespoons) for 30-40 seconds. (See picture ❷)

③ Preheat frying-pan. Cook shrimp with oil (1 1/2 tablespoons) until it turns pink. (picture ❸) Add vegetables and Yoshi's Teriyaki Sauce. Cook for 20 seconds. (See picture ❹)

④ Mix 1 teaspoon cornstarch with 1 ounce of water. Add 1/2 starch mixture to vegetable mixture. (See picture ❺)

⑤ Place on plate and serve.

Makes 1 serving.

Stir Fry Bean Sprouts

Ingredients:

1	cup Bean Sprouts
1	tablespoon Oil
5	tablespoons Yoshi's Teriyaki Sauce
1	leaf Green Lettuce

① Sauté bean sprouts with oil. (See picture ❶)

② Add Yoshi's Teriyaki Sauce when bean sprouts turn from white to clear. (See picture ❷)

③ Cook for 40 seconds or until lightly brown.

④ Place lettuce on plate. Place bean sprouts over the lettuce.

Makes 1 serving.

Note: Recommend cooking at high temperature.

☞ Did you know...

that in Japan the numbers 4 & 9 are considered unlucky? The number 4 in Japanese is pronounced "shi" which sounds the same as the word for death, the number 9 is pronounced "ku" which sounds just like "suffering". So if you go to Japan, don't expect your hotel to have rooms or floors numbered 4, 9 or 13 (which is universally unlucky!).

Stir Fry Bean Sprouts

Stir Fry Green Beans

Ingredients:

2	cups Green Beans
2	tablespoons Oil
6	tablespoons Yoshi's Teriyaki Sauce

① Stem green beans. (See picture ❶)

② Sauté green beans with oil. (See picture ❷)

③ Add Yoshi's Teriyaki Sauce. (See picture ❸)

④ If you prefer more teriyaki taste, cook until brown. (See picture ❹)

⑤ Place on plate and serve.

Makes 2 servings.

Origami (The Ancient Japanese Art of Paper Folding)
The Cicada

①

Start with a square sheet
of paper and fold it
diagonally. Follow dotted
lines and crease and fold.

②

Crease then
fold up points.

③

Fold up along dotted line.

④

Fold along dotted line
toward back.

⑤

And now your
cicada is ready to
fly.

Stir Fry Green Beans

Swordfish Oven Roast

Ingredients:

1	Potato
1	Swordfish steak (12oz.)
1/4	cup Green Beans
1	tablespoon White Wine
6	tablespoons Yoshi's Teriyaki Sauce

① Cut potato in large pieces and boil; do not over cook. (See Picture **❶**)

② Place swordfish, green beans and potatoes in casserole dish. (See Picture **❷**)

④ Add white wine and Yoshi's Teriyaki Sauce. Heat oven to 360 degrees. Bake 20 to 30 minutes uncovered. (See Picture **❸**)

③ Place on plate and serve.

Makes 1 serving.

Note: If fish is cooked this way, there will be less fish odor in your home.

Holidays & Festivals...

Ganjitsu (January 1): New Year's! Nobody works on the first three days of the new year, the period called *sanga nichi*, or *shogatsu*. On these days, people go to shrines, visit friends and relatives, drink sake and eat special new-year dishes like *ozoni* (Japanese soup with rice cakes). *Shimenawa*, sacred rice-straw ropes and pine boughs or *kadomatsu* (gate pines) are hung across gateways. These pine decorations are left up until the seventh of January, a period of time referred to as *matsu no uchi*.

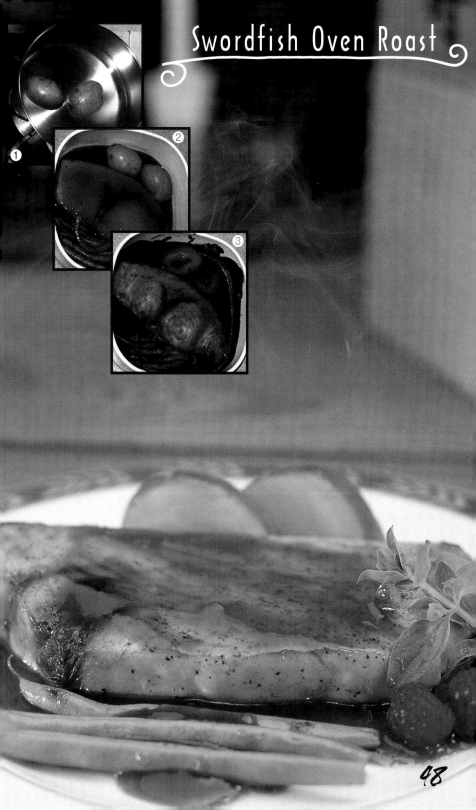

Swordfish Oven Roast

Tofu Teriyaki Steak

Ingredients:

4	slices Tofu
1	cup bean sprouts
2	tablespoons Oil
5	tablespoons Yoshi's Teriyaki Sauce
3	leaves Green Leaf Lettuce
4	sliced Tomatoes
4	bite sized pieces of Broccoli
	Mustard or horseradish

① Cut tofu into 5/8 inch strips. Remove water from Tofu with paper towel. (See picture ❶)

② Sauté bean sprouts with oil (1 tablespoon); When bean sprouts turn its color from white to clear, pour 4 tablespoons of Yoshi's Teriyaki sauce on the sprouts and stir for 40 seconds. For reference see stir fry bean sprout recipe on page 43.

③ Pan fry tofu with oil (1 tablespoon) until brown. Add rest of Yoshi's Teriyaki Sauce. (See picture ❷)

④ Place on plate and serve.

Makes 2 servings.

Tofu Teriyaki Steak

Teriyaki BBQ

Ingredients:

3	Beef Steaks
2 1/2	lbs Chicken with bones
2	Potatos
2	ears Corn
	Salt
	Pepper
3/4	cup Yoshi's Teriyaki Sauce

① Cut potato and corn into preferred sizes. (See picture ❶)

② Place potato and corn into separate pots with water. Cook until done. (test with bamboo stick or fork to check doneness. See picture ❷). When done, sprinkle with 1 teaspoon of salt, wait thirty seconds and then drain.

③ Cut beef steak into preferred size or slice. (See picture ❸) Cut chicken into preferred size. Also slice into thickest parts of chicken so that it will cook more quickly (See picture ❹). Sprinkle salt and pepper on meat.

④ Place beef in a bowl and add 1/4 cup Yoshi's Teriyaki Sauce. Mix well and grill until done. (See picture ❺) Grill chicken without sauce, this is to prevent the chicken from burning. Dip chicken in sauce as it grill and repeat as needed (See picture ❻). Finish the corn and potato by grilling them slightly to add flavor.

Makes 4 servings.

Teriyaki Steak

Ingredients:

8 oz Beef Steak
2 oz Sugar Snap Peas
1/2 medium size Potato
    Salt
    Pepper
1 teaspoon Oil
6 tablespoons Yoshi's Teriyaki Sauce

① Cut potato (See picture ❶).

② Place potato in cold water and cook until done (check to see if it's done by poking with a bamboo stick or fork).

③ Remove extra fat from the steak. Sprinkle with salt and pepper. (See pictures ❷ & ❸)

④ Cook boiled potato with 1/2 tablespoon of oil to brown. (See picture ❹)

⑤ Cook peas with 1/2 tablespoon of oil. Add 1/2 tablespoon Yoshi's Teriyaki Sauce. (See picture ❺) Place potato and peas on the plate.

⑥ Heat frying pan. Cook beef to taste (at least 7 minutes). Add Yoshi's Teriyaki Sauce. Flip over a couple of times to cover the steak with sauce.

Makes 1 serving.

Note: Here is an alternate recipe for kids!

Teriyaki "Saikoro (Dice)" Steak

Ingredients:

8 oz Beef Steak
1/2 cup Bean Sprouts
1/2 cup Spinach
    Salt
    Pepper
2 tablespoon Oil
2 tablespoons Yoshi's Teriyaki Sauce

① Remove extra fat from the steak.
② Cut beef into 3/4 inch cubes.
③ Sprinkle salt and pepper on beef.
④ Sauté bean sprouts with 1 tablespoon of oil. Also sauté spinach with 1 tablespoon of oil. Place both bean sprouts and spinach on plate.
⑤ Cook beef to desired doneness (approx. 5 minutes). Add Yoshi's Teriyaki Sauce and mix well.
⑥ Place beef on plate and serve.

Makes 1 serving.

Teriyaki Steak

Ginger Beef

Ingredients:

8 oz Beef (8 slices - 1oz each)

3/4   cup Zucchini squash

3/4   cup Onion

1/2   tablespoon Ginger

2   teaspoons Oil

5   tablespoons Yoshi's Teriyaki Sauce

---

①   Grate ginger first, then pour 4 tablespoons of Teriyaki Sauce on to ground ginger and mix together. (See picture ❶)

②   Slice 8 oz of beef into eight thin slices. (See picture ❷)

③   Cut zucchini and onion. (See picture ❸)

④   Marinate beef in sauce and ginger mixture. (See picture ❹)

⑤   Preheat frying pan with 1 teaspoon of oil, Sauté vegetables for a minute, then add 1 tablespoon of teriyaki sauce. (See picture ❺) Arrange vegetables on plate.

⑥   Preheat frying pan with 1 teaspoon of oil. Place marinated beef in pan and cook until brown. (See picture ❻)

⑦   Arrange beef on plate with vegetables and serve!

Makes 2 servings.

Ginger Beef

Steamed Rice

Ingredients:

3 cups Rice

Yoshi recommends that you use the equipment as follows:

① See picture ❶
   No. 1: Rice Cooker
   No. 2: Measuring Cup
   No. 3: Large Flat Spoon
   Read instructions for rice cooker
② There are measurement lines in bowl inside the rice cooker to estimate the amount of water needed.
③ Wash rice before cooking. Choose serving size; if you want 4 cups of rice, you need to pour water to level 4 on measurement line in rice cooker's bowl. Please remember, the amount of water you need all depends on the type of rice you cook. (The first time follow directions, then adjust the water as needed.)

Types of rice:
There are two different types of rice.
① Long Grain Rice - usually tastes dry after cooking. For example, rice used in Chinese restaurants. (See A)
② Short Grain Rice - usually sticky after cooking. For example, rice used for sushi. (See B)
③ Yoshi recommends washing rice 20-30 times or until clean. Place rice and water in cooker. Turn on until cooked.
④ Fluff rice before serving.

Note: Rice Cooker can be purchased at most department stores in housewares departments or at many oriental food stores.

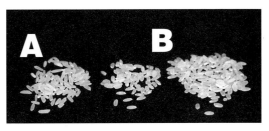

To help recreate the dynamic tastes of Japan, Yoshi has created these sauces so that you too can turn any meal into an event!

To order sauces, tear off page and fill in information and mail, or call the numbers listed below. For your convenience you can also shop via our website located at http://www.argocentury.com/.

Ordering Information

There are three convenient ways to Order:
1. Fill in the form below and send by mail.
2. To order by fax: (704) 525-6280 or (800) 446-7131.
3. Or please call: (800) 446-7108.

To Order by mail...

Name: _____

Address: _____

City: _____ State: _____ ZIP: _____

Tel #: _(_____)_____

I would like to order:

      _____ Yoshi's Ginger Dressing   _____ Yoshi's Teriyaki Dressing

      _____ Yoshi's Super Teriyaki Sauce

$4.95 for each bottle ordered.

Shipping:

Order Total	Add	Order Total	Add	Order Total	Add
$20 or less	$6	$45.01 - 60	$9	$99.01 - 125	$12
$20.01 - 30	$7	$60.01 - 75	$10	$125 or more	10%
$30.01 - 45	$8	$75.01 - 99	$11		

Methods of payment: __ Amex/Diners   __ Mastercard   __ VISA   __ Check

Credit card number: _____ Exp. Date: _____

Name as it appears on card: _____

Please remove page, fold and enclose in an envelope and mail to address listed on back or fold and tape or staple and apply appropriate postage.

Argo Century Inc. / U.S.A.
4603 South Blvd.
Charlotte, NC 28209